A Broken Heart Can Kill You

Kenya Smith
A Broken Heart Can Kill You

All rights reserved
Copyright © 2023 by Kenya Smith

No part of this publication may be reproduced, distributed, or transmitted in any form or by any means, including photocopying, recording, or other electronic or mechanical methods, without the prior written permission of the publisher, except in the case of brief quotations embodied in critical reviews and certain other noncommercial uses permitted by copyright law.

Published by BooxAI

ISBN: 978-965-578-055-0

A Broken Heart Can Kill You
Love and Lost Poems for the New World

KK Rice

I Remember

I remember when we loved so deeply,

it shook the earth and heavens frequently,

we never gave the gods a chance.

We held each other and proceeded

to mock them with our romance.

As we dared to be together without pause.

Making new laws the two of us soared to new heights

with the passionate awe of neophytes,

who never found the love to even last one night?

You said, may the color of red,

surround our souls once a year at least and

honor love again counting every decade hence.

I will save the suspense; I refuse to relent on the idea of loving you.

I plan every day no matter what you say, to keep you.

My favorite part is when they say look at those two.

Moving your hair out of your face, kissing you so deeply,

I can only trace the feeling I had, back when we said I love you.

Never holding each other to the pact.

Too late, I discovered how closely I am attached.

And when you left, I had to unpack how to lose you.

Now I am an empty man... complete with no plan with a burned down soul.

Having no talent to speak or cajole any love from you...

my ravaged heart torn in two,

each piece will burn forever...

but only for you.

KK Rice

Push

I don't want to feel like I am pushing you away...

not anymore, not in any way.

I see that when I try to move closer...

more distance for us is pushed forward.

I feel like a freeloader on your time

and your heart, I only want to start,

to heal the chasm between our souls.

Over our time I never really told. How much I love you so.

I need to unload the weight of guilt I feel when I speak your name...

when you left me I was never quite the same.

It was only with you, did I ever feel the flames of burning love and desire.

I wanted your fire. To keep my heart warm...

But my love was a thorn in your side.

Once removed... you began to fly. I finally recognized.

It was right what you said the day that you left...

I was seeing red, through my tears.

I began to dread the emptiness I always feared...

I wasn't right. No need to fight the truth.

We both knew the route of mistaken love or just pure lust...

we couldn't really trust our blood under a rush to fill our desire.

Yes, I still love that fire...

but it proves to only misfire over my plans

to make you feel whole.

How to fit the pieces with you is my goal.

KK Rice

Beautiful Dream

What a beautiful feeling given to me when in my dream,

you loved me. Love with you was a beautiful scene.

Something special in my beautiful dream.

I could not have foreseen to capture

what had been given to me.

I want and not have to hide.

To show the world my new pride.

With my eyes now wide.

Watching others struggle and wrestle.

With feelings they had deep inside.

But never taking the chance,

to see if their love will abide.

Not knowing what to do.

When an angel has finally looked at you.

No longer timid or shy... just prepared to fly.

My eyes now want to cry, because I was no longer denied.

The dream revealed we laughed

and looked into each other's eyes.

All the while our souls merged,

we listened to pathetic sighs... from those.

Green with thought and others wrought,

with their venomous words for our fall.

The dream ends and I am awake.

Thanking god for my fate.

I made my life beautiful before I was too late.

Rolling over to kiss you as my beautiful dream

had long ago come true...

KK Rice

Miss Her

Often, I think but I can't still see.

Why she'll see him but not see me.

I hope she knows I miss her too.

It's not a feeling reserved to that other dude.

I know she wants to protect her heart...

I was wrong with her from the very start.

Given that I still care for you...

like any man I need to be fed too.

I see the pictures that you display.

Of happy times you have anyway...

you think of me as a fool.

You not really caring, while I am still missing you...

I guess what my heart is telling me is true.

You left me. I didn't leave you. But this I won't defend.

I honestly admit. You picked up and walked and didn't trip.

I think I can give you credit you know.

You did it right away and not even slow.

You made up your mind and that was completely it.

No longer would I be allowed to kiss your lips.

Or touch your hand. I know it's true.

You gave me my papers to leave you.

Alone you prefer. Please don't disturb...

the life you are living best... with the people you can rest your guard...

from pain or disregard from me.

My life is a mess... I can't give you my best...

even if I miss your voice... I miss your lips. I wasn't given a choice.

I miss the love you won't admit you gave.

You shake your head while walking away.

I was a fool. I made a mistake.

That wasn't you. You needed respect...

I can't eat cake twice. You put me in check...

you told me take my punishment and keep it deep in my chest.

I learned how a lonely heart felt... so I sat and accepted

the cards I was dealt. I felt dead all the way to my heart as they say.

Knowing that my love couldn't

at least be given away...

KK Rice

Crazy Life

A crazy life... I like despite...

all the challenges that strain me...

What is life without the strife.

The life that could be unfulfilling.

I dream to create the plan

of a life that is inspiring.

I can make a mark. Change the dark.

Enlighten those who can't see.

To form ideas that may cause fears from those

hearts that will not know me...

From those who fear. The first

you hear of a road unpaved

to a new truth revealing.

Nevertheless, I work my best

for a new world less belittling.

KK Rice

You

My god, I never seen anything like you but in a dream.

In my dream there was only two...

walking thru heaven me and you.

Holding your hand in desperate embrace.

That you would choose me to be in your space.

I can't believe I have you in my life,

if someone asked, I would say it's a lie.

I could never aspire to possess such fire and light.

Like to the center of the universe,

such a distance I would transverse.

With better odds and certainly risk,

better the risk than to totally miss.

The opportunity to have you this day,

but you may walk away to my utter dismay.

I look at my hands like holding sand

with fingers outstretched.

Despite my anguished protest,

my scream grotesque, as you simply slipped away.

KK Rice

Love Gave You to Me

What love has given me. Is a tale.

Told many times it becomes stale.

What was different when I met you.

My heart told me I was through.

My eyes filled with the sight of you.

My spirit wanted to fight for you.

I can't remember how many times

I wanted the scent of your skin. In my mind.

Locked away with my sins.

I watched you move with silent pride.

Knowing everyone was feeling your stride,

even with my heart shredded

I couldn't let you go I admitted.

Let down my wall to create a hole

through which everything I had was stolen.

You reached so far into me...

I was breathing, yes, but just barely...

Never have I fallen so fast so hard.

You've scrambled my life thus far,

I haven't been the same ever since,

I lost my mind even against my wish.

There was no way I could not fall for you.

Your eyes and lips ended that ruse.

And today I stand a slightly broken man

with no tales to prove.

I was once so happy with you.

Loving you every day as I proposed,

I hope you know

we still reap what we sow.

KK Rice

Away

What did I say for you to go away?
How did I speak so that you would seek another way?

Only my heart loves your rage in my soul weeps forever
because you would not stay.

To the devil I met. And I would pay
my eternal soul in the parlay.

My words to you only decay the false wall
of indifference in my way.

My love would leave most in dismay,
not believing. I can feel this way.

About one soul. I mean you.
If I can be so bold.

KK Rice

Consistency

Did I do that? Did I cause a scene?

I can't have your love. Because I have no…

Consistency…

My love hasn't changed, or become

deranged, or given you pain.

Consistency…

Listen to me. I know my heart not always pure.

I know your love provides the cure…

Your eyes and lips are my lure.

Consistency…

I know I am evil… to think you so feeble.

I write to you so you can have.

Consistency…

My heart wishes upon a star.

Your heart won't change who you are.

I hope what I feel will leave a scar.

Consistency…

I can be hurt 1000 times…

I know it's insane.

The benefit is this pain you give me

is all mine.

Consistency…

KK Rice

I Write For You

I could write for you every day...

I string the words then I pray.

That you feel my heart in prose.

And send you love to get rid of your woe.

All these words are designed for your soul.

I hope you feel they never get old.

On days you feel as no one really cares for you.

Read all these words so you know it not true.

I see your image and... I just begin...

to find the words that I hope make you grin.

Your small smile means I touched a heart.

My first and only wish from the start.

KK Rice

With Him

The truth is and I won't admit.

Is that my life alone just doesn't fit?

The missing clues are very crude...

I made it all up when I saw you with that dude.

I wanted to commit…

acts of wanton lust but you are not doing anything until you trust...

I understand you want love too.

Not just someone to make your life a zoo.

How lost I was after you left, with the girls for the night.

All dressed, in pearls and new hairlights.

Looking and checking my IG for any signs if I dare.

Seeing the images, there is that same dude, big as life.

Smiling and sweating was his way, obviously seeing his head under the waves.

Out of his league when being with you.

Nothing I say, can change the way.

I constantly curse the time you spend with him.

If I could, it would be a sin. Or is it a crime?

But that don't rhyme. Why I am trying to claim

what isn't mine. Looking at my time left,

trying to decide what is best for my torn heart.

I forgot. Be smart. Don't proceed, don't start,

in the world forbidden, where you can't win.

You start to see what you begin,

not really feeling the pain of the wind.

KK Rice

Who

Who held you close and danced all night?

Who whispered in your ear and prayed at first sight?

How many hearts raced when you arrived?

Who grabbed your hips to feel your stride?

Who held your waist to feel the rhythm of heaven?

Give me the names they are all dead men.

How many men heart's broke in an instant?

How many pleas became insignificant?

You are an angel and quite magnificent.

Your whisper to know your name is what they seek.

Recognizing their forked tongues as they speak.

How do your feet float above the ground?

You approach the heart without making a sound.

KK Rice

New York-1 Prologue

I remember New York, before the mask.

When the main concern was the task,

of daily survival on the train.

Catching a cab in the rain...

Getting to work by 9.

Pretending the workload was fine.

6 pm link up so the boys can pick up warm up drinks,

walking the street past the food garbage that stinks.

Hearing the sirens from the EMS so loud.

Hitting 58th street to hang out at Tao.

Later that night W 8th floor...

Later still see you at Marquee at the door.

I remember what it is like.

To shop just right.

Start at 59th street and descend on 5th Ave left to right.

BG to LV to DC all quite lovely.

Though it gets complex, Rolex or Omega.

What is your Net, worth the time to find another way to spend your dime.

There is no mask... so let us walk to,

MSG where the Knicks are crushing the court.

Yes, only the corporate box will do,

drinking beers with client, when payments are due.

I miss the old New York what can it be?

Probably the people diversity.

So many tongues from immigrant sons and

daughters of the 1st New Yorkers passed.

Creating a culture of mixed influences and traditions smashed

together so now it's cool. New York can't follow while it is making the rules.

Spreading our dreams to people who are not fools.

KK Rice

Black

The world went black,

I settled back

into my lack of ambition.

Lost so much speed,

I did indeed,

lose my momentum.

Myself, still lost I bear the cross

to give my ID attention.

Although I sleep to noon or three.

I still need the connection to my creations.

Although I don't see or no longer need the work to be perfection,

life will soon breathe, and I will conceive for myself a new direction.

The life before, created a chore. For my sense of well-being.

I never admitted my life I can't figure,

all at once it can be a bitter bore.

Constantly changing while still aging.

Let me shape forward to make myself look like a rose.

There is one certainty, I need this before I am one with eternity.

KK Rice

Try

Try as I might how little I can write

without your spirit to inspire me.

I take pen to hand and make

a grand plan to write words that are poetry.

What I didn't realize is how much you provide,

and now I surmise that your

beautiful soul is what influences me.

Think as I must, despite my new trust in my abilities.

I realize too late it a matter of fate

that pain of not seeing you moves me.

And now I am in relief unlike a thief.

The words flow freely to me.

I am glad I found the plentiful fountain

of feelings for you that has continuously guided me.

What a humorous turn with this time I learned

that not having you is why I write poetry.

KK Rice

The Day

I remember the day…

You were right to walk away.

I couldn't give you the right words to stay...

You left to return to what you hold dear.

I made the error... to only give you fear.

A sweet little devil was speaking in my ear...

To tell you all you wanted to hear... only your back

I saw through my tear. The quick clicks of your heels…

Still echo in my ear... I could not even catch you.

Your female scent became a venom in my vein...

I miss you so much... it makes me insane...

You were right to leave me standing...

Only with my pain... my last vision of you.

Walking away.

KK Rice

New York 2

New York Love is different you will see it's true.

Loving is easy that's what folks do.

Loving you and the light bill. Would be great too.

I get rid of them chicks I claim to repent.

Listen to my love, because we still got rent.

Love in New York is a difficult course.

If work becomes my first love, then I have lost.

The love we have is crazy just like that glue.

Yes, it starts to faze me to be without you.

Hand in hand we walk to the subway by the bridge.

Mouthwatering over the leftovers in the fridge.

The meal is always great on the next night.

Sit on my lap drink red wine on the next bite...

scoop you up in my tired arms.

Letting you know you will never be harmed.

KK Rice

Struggle

You asked me once... what if we...

made the leap together... to be free...

what if we had taken that chance...

to love each other with deep romance...

Where would we be... under a tree?

Sharing the fruit bared from thee?

Would we be cursed?

Or even worse, blessed from our treachery.

We were bonded by heart alone to the others we never shown

our true intentions, we never mentioned we traded hearts...

not to start a chat or random thoughts.

How could it be? How they can love?

So free, with hearts so entangled constantly?

No room to breathe or even walk.

Out the home without a talk. Keep your heart in your chest.

Don't take a rest. Never consider, if this was best,

take a deep breath... always the depth...

(Of Dante's 2nd ring...)

Never forget. With this in our essence how can we want

To be in each other presence.

We talk together well... we shoulder the weight of other

people's hell.

We are strong in ways that others don't understand.

We are the same creature whatever the plan.

With this I proposed that one day we find a sympathy to compose.

And rewrite all our previous plans. The ones without us. I just can't stand.

We gave too much of our hearts it's a sin, not to live to the fullest.

I believe the Gods that love want us to win.

It's time to start chapter 2 of this book... with a title

"They made this all work."

KK Rice

Love-1

Love can it be? To never feel alone.

To allow all our weakness to frankly be shown.

To remove the false cover of the unknown.

Freely look at me with all your judgements and insecurities.

Test me and see. What I want to be. In love with you.

Till all is gone and we begin anew.

Keep my heart close to you. Know that you own me.

Yes, it is true nothing can keep me from loving you.

Everything that I could possibly be.

Will only be worth eternity when you are with me.

What love can do. Give one the air to try something new.

Give one a chance to get rid of the few.

Give one the strength of a 100 more.

Give one the light to see even more.

Let one see blood to settle the score.

Give one pain to live not one day more.

All these sides of love's eternal cube...

I can only find when I seek you.

My heart... I love you...

KK Rice

Resolve

Your scent has the strength of the summer rain.

It makes me strong I feel no pain.

I need that scent it keeps me sane.

To all my other dears, I must make this plain.

There is only one that captures my heart.

Only one I will make a start.

Only one who makes me a fool.

You tried your best... but it won't be you.

Only her spirit makes me feel alive.

Only for her will I deprive...

my lustful words to other birds who take flight...

the moment things don't seem right...

I plan my goals with certain care.

My final goal is to make a pair.

Two hearts that's me and you...

I've seen your others. I know a few.

They won't love you.

The way I can for certain they don't have a plan...

they will walk away when life gets thick.

Look around to only pick... someone lesser than you

of course.

They won't realize the remorse of

Seeing you back in my space...

and hold your hand...

and I am glad I planned...

Patience has a smiling face.

KK Rice

Talk With Son

Time is life. That truth is known.

What is not as seen or clearly shown...

how time some days played me for a fool...

from this I formed some simple tools...

Men think time is their friend.

They think it's a road that has no end,

or even worse, there is more

road around the bend.

Sit my son let us speak on time.

You ask is it a crooked walk or a straight line.

Is it a crawl through thickets so sharp and unfeeling or

is it in the air ready to do men's bidding?

What can I teach you my son?

Now that I know the truth...

How do I help you find the brightest route?

My desire as an original son... to teach my own some simple points.

First, don't ever turn your head or blink in the light...

Blind yourself in the blessing of insight.

Next, let the tears you produce now...

reduce the years that you lose in regret that you choose the life undefined.

Lastly, fate will let you stand in line for the life not divine.

I can only speak my son, only you in the end to digest

that what we discussed...

even if my words lead to your slumber,

you must. Resolve yourself into a future you trust.

KK Rice

Waiting

I miss the night. We were right.

I fell in love with you so quickly.

Your lips and your hair.

I couldn't dare not to love you completely.

I watched you dance I was in a trance.

I saw a future that was risky...

My heart ensnared.

My soul didn't care.

I was blind blissfully.

Out of control... you were taking a toll

on my heart, definitely.

Kissing your hand, I couldn't stand

to see you without me...

A bitter loss, my love is tossed,

to the side and a life that will never be...

I know this is the truth, I will follow the route.

To a place less frightening...

Deep in my heart...

we will never be apart...

I will be... waiting to hear

hopefully for the day when your full soft lips request me.

KK Rice

Rise To The Truth

What is this I feel?

My pain real...

it rings in my ears...

amongst my tears.

When did I become this lie?

What is a day like?

Without those dark clouds in the sky?

And the ones with those evil eyes...

That seem to look in my soul...

my spirit is lost...

I have nothing left to hold,

I wrap myself in a blanket of sad...

Perhaps only wishing...

for what I once had...

a thought I wished...

to dream in reverse...

Correct those ills...

I once rehearsed.

A younger man feels no fear I know

he dances like a fool.

Because he thinks life is slow...

he didn't think to make his mark...

before his life enters the dark...

grasp early the fruits of life...

Love the one who makes you right.

Hold tight to the desires of the heart...

not just what this small world

around you has taught…

KK Rice

The Crush

He waits with the feeling

of a nervous schoolboy

to carry her books home from school...

She can only see the charm of a man

disarmed by the beauty she gave.

Thus, give him the chance now for romance.

If he behaves.

His love is thirst, his heart will burst, like a

volcano for 1000 years from this day.

KK Rice

The Recovery

Alone I sit...

with pills equipped...

To give me life,

undeserving.

I took a stance,

not really a chance.

To find that which would

complete me...

Although your touch

was never too much.

I succeeded in time. To consider it mine.

Foolishly...

One might as well wish

for an extended kiss

from those who would

curse me.

My heart will one day cease,

to give one more beat...

but it will never defeat.

The alone part that you gave me.

KK Rice

Red

When I envision your form.

I see a beautiful rose.

Red so powerful.

It moves my soul.

The power of your scent that lingers and scars my heart...

at night my dream is for your touch to leave a mark...

the curves of your lips and your eyes

make some despise your existence.

I can't see what they feel.

It makes no sense...

they have never held your hand or felt your embrace.

Or walked in your warmth, style or grace.

I continue to be a fool to your dominance on my mind.

I breathe your name while I give my sorrowful sighs...

how such a feeling for you has shaped my thoughts.

I realized if my time comes again.

I will have swiftly fought.

For the most powerful force ever sought...

the attention of your heart.

For this it is never for naught.

KK Rice

Live With It

You are gone.

That is my fate.

I look at the world and try not to hate.

I long for your whisper ending with "you".

So, I can quickly reply what I feel too.

Your beating heart when I hold you.

I miss... how quickly it beats when we would kiss.

Knowing you love someone never ends

even when you decide to be friends.

But then of course I miss that too.

When you hear my name you mostly say who?

It ok to try... to forget your eyes...

Though they haunt me so. I never know...

when I will love you again... you will never bend.

I must accept my loss. Of feelings tossed to the wind.

KK Rice

Sidewinder

Inside I'm loss. It still my fault.

To let my life, go this way.

I still entrust... to luck and stakes...

to find my eventual fate.

Even my love.

That once was great...

remains only as a taste...

of a past unfound.

How crude it sounds.

To let so much go to waste...

the sun will shine... while many whine...

that they cannot stand the light.

We must learn to trust...

control our lust. For the few things we think make us free.

But our eternal thirst for the certain lurch...

toward our desires will always be.

KK Rice

The Why

Try as I might how little I can write,
without your spirit to inspire me...
I take pen to hand and make a grand plan to write
words that are poetry.

What I didn't realize, is how much your
beautiful soul is what influences me.
I this truth but still dig deep in my roots
despite my trust in my abilities.

I realize too late it is a matter of fate that pain
of not seeing you moves me.
And now I am in relief unlike a thief.
The words flow freely to me.

I am glad I found the plentiful fountain
of feelings for you that has continuously guided me.
What a humorous turn with this time I learned
that not having you is why I write poetry.

KK Rice

The Watching

I watch the electronic feeds the modern

world gives us the truth we need.

All I can see is you with him

having a good time living to win.

I see the smiles and tender feel of

hands pressed together with no repeal.

Holding your hips dance all night

kissing your lips all within sight.

Speaking the words. I am sure end with "You"

taking the time to stay in the mood.

Now I'm fixed like a dear on the road

how stay mixed in "My" business mode.

I can't comment on your happy life...

I think it prudent for him to make you his wife.

Nothing wrong... nothing to judge. It up to me if I hold a grudge.

Just mad at myself. Nothing to do with you...

I had a chance for a moment but didn't see it through...

didn't want to be dirty didn't try to stay clean...

but life comes harshly if you don't say what you mean.

And back that up still... with iron will... and sleep in the grave you made.

That completely makes the story less vexed and perhaps even more truthfully made.

KK Rice

When We First Met,

I had no idea my heart could burst.

Every day since I think of you first.

I remember that day with clear ambition.

There are other times in my mind I still unpack.

With something as simple as kissing your back.

The way you moved your hair to the side.

So, I would not miss your scent inside my mind.

I spoiled you then I believe,

I think you knew you had me up your sleeve.

And the day came when you left.

Walking away I only felt death, and my soul became grey.

I have never filled the void with another.

Only my memories of you roll in like thunder.

My tears are lost that is plain to see.

So many drops in the vast sea.

KK Rice

Work For My Son

I am tired son, the day is done,

I am coming home but cannot run.

My hands did work moving dirt so that

I can bring some money home.

Your mom and me do the work of three and

would add four to bring home more to be sure you have all you need.

We don't have much but you can trust that we will die

before we give up making sure you have enough.

Your dad moves dirt. Your mom washes shirts

with great pride and consistency.

We up at dawn with a yawn

in our mind we just suck it up.

When dusk thus comes, we are done

with aching fingers and swollen feet.

The sun sets, we have not wept, because we provided

what we need to live and eat.

Cash and gold don't always show

the pride in the honorable heart.

But hard work pays in many ways, more when

pride in your work gives you your respect from the start.

KK Rice

Love 3

I am meeting my fate.

The destiny I created.

Only by chance or risk of my heart and my soul.

You had long said the words that I dread...

you don't love me anymore.

I took a chance to find a stance on which to try to love you more.

But time is revealing.

I was only stealing

what little heart I could hold.

I completely confess to the theft I won't rest.

Until I possess your entire soul.

My heart is blind so I crossed the line to a place that my love for you couldn't resist.

It's from there that I miss

your hair and your lips,

which part to tell me. Don't stare.

KK Rice

Happy

One day I swear I will never impair your goal to leave me.

I will let go. I will no longer tow this bond I hold so desperately...

I must make it true, less I rue,

the days stretched before me.

I must now accept you no longer love this

wretched soul that has become me.

I danced around to make it sound that there

was an opportunity before me.

Too late it is. To create a quiz, that will test your

loyalty to me. You have none, though I

considered it fun, to pretend one day

we would have a long history.

Not a slight chance, for my love to advance

with you beneficially. Every night I gaze, at the picture

I saved of you and I being happy.

Though try as I might truth is in sight.

That the only one truly happy was me.

KK Rice

The Island To Have Love

I want to find an island where I can be alone with you.

A special place far away, where our love

would be our food. For drink we can lay

in each other's arms and quench our thirst, in sweat

immersed in passion fueled tequila and rum drinks that are fun.

Oh yes, feel the warm sand

on our feet as we run.

Into the sunset of bright orange hues.

I hold your hand and tell you that I love you.

Then I hold you tight.

We have so much love that we make it all night.

In the morning you are still here. I watch the sun

while playing with your hair. Knowing all is right.

I am happy that I got to hold you all night.

Please tell me I have you all for eternity.

One day maybe we will be free...

I'm taking it on faith that this will be our reality.

Come let us pray, the world will parlay

for our love to be complete

and never thrown away.

KK Rice

My Boy

My lord... my joy. To be the father of a boy.

I stand before him as he looks up at me,

I see in him all the potential that missed me.

I held my son for the first time to see...

my nose my face even my feet.

Knowing he will grow up to be the better version of me...

I want to guide the eventual king.

I only pray... I will come to see...

the wisdom passed to him,

as it was passed to me.

To see him grow to his fifty.

To see his kids, gather at his feet.

To look at their dad over six feet.

He will be a giant in their eyes and eventually see...

the love that makes us a family tree...

Beware my son. Try to be sweet.

The world will be cruel and often bleak.

Keep your heart and your mind as clean as can be.

Teach the next generation better than me.

Where I failed, I beg you to succeed.

Any oak has many leaves.

Be strong like that and you will see...

The strength of your love is all you need.

KK Rice

Forever

Like a fire burning through my soul.

The world would not be as beautiful.

If you were not so bold.

From the light of ancient star.

The legend has been told.

Nothing as true as you

has ever been controlled.

From a forked tongue many lies have been sold.

Nevertheless, my love for you will forever hold.

KK Rice

Consequences

I wish I could go back in time.

When the love in my heart would not be a crime.

I see your smile in pictures of old.

I always wonder what you were told.

The time lost will never come back.

My regrets in life have carved my paths.

To move to the left or the right...

My only wish is you were in my sight.

To hold on to your heart with all my might.

But that wouldn't be dignified.

KK Rice

Please Forgive

What does forgiveness mean?

Does it mean that we no longer harbor ill feelings?

Or no longer hold others to be accountable

for the pain or hurt they have given?

Does it mean we have forgotten the sickness of our neighbor's irregulars?

Have we passed our internal evil out of

our soul, clean our mind of

stagnant water and blood?

Do we let our hearts ring free of revenge?

Or do we plot, for the day we will avenge.

Forgiveness is an act that is divine, it not natural from our small minds.

If you can master this, you will find a life complete.

A feeling so good it will run deep. If this is lost to you.

Then you have failed, and, in your hate,

you will find only hell.

KK Rice

Black Sight

Why do I only see everything black?

What is it in my life that I lack?

Every day, when I wake, my sight only takes

on the darkness and not the light.

I beg the lord for more insight

the hole in my heart has been filled by the dark

if I knew better, I would discard these

feelings of black that corrupt as I began.

Not this man, that walks to purport a feeling

of hope for a brighter future, with this toll...

I feel the blackness, but I can't let go.

Don't show, the world outside what I tow.

Internally, though nobody cares... no one

shares the light, hold tight. Not taking any

love to fight the fight.

Of our lives is maybe our demise.

That why the dark coincides with the

loss of the light we can feel... what on

earth is real? Family, friends, making ends,

then life ends.

Never does the blackness end.

To encompass all within our soul...

sooner or later becomes the mold for living a life I stole.

From my favorite TV show. Last night, I discovered this fright...

I realized the waste that I know.

Right now, it's just a sin. How you doing? How you been?

All the people crowd around as if I have been,

something new to them...

They only want me so they can win…
once I see through the blackness,
I will lack less of the shroud
I've been proud to call indifference.

I'm tense. All I've seen because
I now bear witness. Remove the dark,
start a spark, my best girl at the park,
putting my name in the oak tree bark.

There it stays for all days...
they all circle me just like
a maze. Left or right.
Remember no sight.

KK Rice

Reach

I got to live to see the light.

Reach above and pull it down.

Wear it just like a crown.

I was lost but now I am right.

My pure soul gave the fight.

The blackness ends and now bends to my will.

What do I intend to do with my

new lease on life?

Remember to capture the light,

fight the dark. Don't give an inch

despite the pinch, I can feel the hangman's lynch.

Escaped again cause life won't end.

Until the blackness wins.

KK Rice

All I need

Your arms around me

is all I need to be happy

more than I ever believed.

Your kiss on my head is all

I need to feel I am yours for all to see.

The look in your eyes is all

I need to know I can love, and we can be free.

The kiss of your lips is all I need

to live in this world and know

I am first in your needs.

The feel of your hand is all

I need to feel that my heart no longer bleeds.

The sound of your voice is all I need

to feel like I will never want you away from me.

The beauty of your soul is all

I need to feel once again that I can breathe.

If you say I love you, it is all I need

to believe that is true indeed.

KK Rice

That Night

There was the night you were so beautiful

it was unfathomable that you could be seen with me.

I never will forget how you brought fire to the scenery.

Watching you dressed in red that night

fed my heart and soul just right...

Your hair was so soft and captured the light,

your eyes I love, I would gaze

in your eyes even if I was looking at hell.

Your lips have curves of beautiful flowers

I've preserved the memory of kissing them for hours...

Even as our relationship got cold and sour.

Distance persisted each of our wrongs

clearly listed, twisted and

slightly mislead. I want to rethread the eye

of the needle of your heart.

Just tell me where to start.

I want to begin to win your love back...

even if the odds are stacked against me.

Convince me. We don't have a solid history.

For the two of us to find victory...

A meeting of two thoughtful minds.

We'll leave all the mess behind.

So, we waste no more time.

Let me discover a convincing line.

Give me the time again to make you mine.

KK Rice

My Dream Awaken

Did I ever tell you you're my dream?

Like heaven on earth just a queen.

I never seen someone so beautiful,

you are one of kind it would seem.

Which is why you are always trapped in my dreams.

In real life you flew away. I had to let you go. You wouldn't stay.

You needed something more and that's ok...

I couldn't compete with my love to my dismay.

Just a man in love so I say.

You roll eyes and wave me away.

I couldn't give you anything in a parlay.

Love is more than words, you say.

I became as nothing when you went away.

Your hair and lips. Your eyes and hips.

Your skin and scent trapped in mind and it will stay.

Become that man, you would say.

I been working to this day.

To become more worthy of your love.

Don't move me away from your soul.

Hearts don't come easy to mold.

My heart belongs to you. Which was stolen.

From some poor old dude on the lonely road...

yeah, I am that old dude truth be told.

It was me lonely walking on the road... playing games.

You swear this is what drove you insane.

That why you got on that plane...

leaving me crying at gate 8,

yes, it was a shame.

In your new world, you became,

a total new person with a good name...

Now we all look in your light, the world has yet to see such a sight.

With you at all you might, there is no night anymore,

because you are so bright. You just soar.

Dealing with our love, for you, was a fucking chore.

Next time I see you I'll start a war.

Don't be shocked, don't be sore.

You always knew

I wanted more.

KK Rice

My Own

Would it be too much ego to say I have cried?

I don't joke. Reading all of poetry that I wrote.

Never have I been so touched but shocked

by what I carry in my heart..

Sad that it seems in all the dreams I am not in this world.

But very far away, put some place else

where my struggle is heartfelt,

and all my pain is taken away.

Though I write this text it was not my intent

to vent to you in any way.

I feel torn apart and not healed,

just dry rot, from so many years of black tears streaming down my face.

I bring it on myself, and this is the result

from so many problems, I backed away.

Never can I stand the hurt and sheer pain

of time and unfortunate days.

KK Rice

Broken But Whole

How to heal... while I wantonly steal
a moment in time with you...
how to hide the dime received from that crime
I used to call you. How to find the time I need to beg
on one knee for your attention.

Did I mention? My heart is thoroughly broken
while you spoke of love in another way.
Obviously, not to play the role you showed
me before running away.
Run if you must in god you trust.

You won't get away... my heart is in tune
to love just you and even blind
I can find you any day...
Or you can desperately try to sneak a slide
to the rear door and never have your clarity.

Run with the wind, yes alone, but that's hardly a sin.
While you miss our beautiful destiny...
Lie if it's right,
I will only hold you tight...
for as long as you allow me...

KK Rice

Forever Beautiful

You ask me if your beauty still stands.

The winds of time and adverse plans

to meet your fate with careless zeal.

To this thought I can only feel,

helpless as a bird looking through a window

at your beautiful form, then I am an eagle.

With the freedom to fly, so high without care

or, more notably, with just a helpless stare.

I cannot conceive how beautiful you are.

Like common men trying to understand the essence of a star.

My words may mark the despair I feel,

when I see you live your life with that zeal.

My only wish is not to watch you conceal

your heart that bleeds.

I hope only for me... which I can heal...

KK Rice

The Constant Believer

Love is lost. She even tossed...

my small soul away... my heart still bleeds...

but you concede...

there could be love one day...

Can we not rethink,

with a kiss and a wink, a far better way.

When one will find... that love is time...

and it all about when you meet.

In Einstein's gaze... of time and space...

love still evaded even he...

for the smartest man should know

to plan for all that love will bring...

One last embrace,

love should give, not take

and will even make, a love believer

once more of me.

KK Rice

I'm Woke

I woke up... I can't rest.

I hate my fate... what a mess...

I think of you. Close to my chest...

If I had thought... we would have made a nest.

Working each day to be our best.

Lucky day.... we passed the test...

Life's not cruel when you get more rest

back to sleep. It was only to depart.

Burning flames in my own torn heart...

KK Rice

The Her

Your beauty is like a warm summer day.

It fuels my loyalty I will not sway.

I dream of days where your beauty is the light.

It eases my pain and warms my night.

If I was able to wish a wish that would instantly come true.

My only wish would be to be with you...

KK Rice

The Devil Is A Fool

Do you know how beautiful you are?

Do you know your eyes shine brighter than the stars?

Do you know that your presence gives me peace?

Do you know that your beauty I always seek?

When I see you, I fall in love once again.

It is circular, there is no beginning and there is no end,

the cycle of being in love with you.

Has clearly made me such a fool.

Now I see clearly, I hope you do too.

Please say you love me always too.

Do you know I don't breathe?

If I am not with you?

Do you know my heart is torn but you're the glue?

Do you know I faced the devil to be with you?

I met Satan way back in June.

He wanted to parlay my soul to be with you.

He said, I'll make a deal with you.

I'll tear your soul in half, that will do.

Your half only belongs to you and

my half will burn in hell, I'll see it through...

But she will always belong to you.

I laughed and cried,

then showed him out.

I was already her property without a doubt.

You have nothing I need. I said.

I'll just wait for her instead.

I said to her, my half I gave to my love. I mean you.

I hope you can see the wound goes all the way through.

I hope your love will make me new.

And now together,

without the devil,

we can be two.

KK Rice

Yeah Right

You really think I won't love you??

Give me some credit.

I am not a fool.

I see what you are, that beautiful star,

I know what you like.

Since we met that beautiful night.

I see your beautiful eyes and

curves of your lips...

I held you close once hip to hip.

I know your soft voice in my ear.

I know how to keep you very near,

PDA's are what I do.

If I didn't, how would you know that I love you?

I see your soft shoulders getting cold.

I kiss your back then attack your full lips.

I am so bold they don't lack my affection towards the truth.

I take your hand, my demand,

we get to the event and we stand for

the pictures and flashes from the fans.

We are two stars.

We need to show them who we are,

wearing your blue and I wear my black.

Listening to all the dudes realizing what they lack.

I love who you are.

I will never step back.

KK Rice

Zoloft

Why can I only cry?
Why do I feel like I must die?
I can't grasp why I feel like this,
empty, useless, and listless?

Why can only cry?
What did I do to get the evil eye?
This curse upon me…
has extracted its fee…

Why can I only cry?
I look at world now only with dead eyes.
Why can I only cry?
Certainly, there is other people eviler than I.

Why can I only cry?
I did everything that I could to just get by.
Why can I only cry?
I ask this more every day that goes by.

Why can I only cry? Dark days surround me,
I can no longer see the sky.
Why can I only cry?
My love has left me, and I think I know why.

Why can I only cry?
Is this what happens right before you die?
Why can I only cry?
I have so much sadness still ahead to absorb inside.

Why can I only cry?
So much time wasted,
I truly despise everything,
taken amid the lies.

Why can I only cry?

I didn't realize. How much I needed you at my side.

Why can I only cry? I need way to fully survive.

Why can I only cry? Deep down inside I'm broken.

I can't deny I been hiding that side.

Why can I only cry?

Simple,

I have depression.

KK Rice

Here And Gone The Heart Is Torn.

I will one day find the formula to move time,
in reverse to avoid the hurt you mercilessly served me.

My heart became alert after I became immersed
in your love then have it taken away, I feel ruthlessly.

You gave me a glimpse and now I sorely miss
everything you may have had to complete me.

I dream every night even if it not right.
Of new ways to love you without weeping.

I will attempt to compel you and to others
do not tell the idea that I will love you.

For just a few minutes a day.
If you can make this time more.

For me to explore my dissent voiced
by the chore of loving you but staying away.

KK Rice

Distance

Please tell me there is another way

I can love you and not chase you away...

Can I find the right words not to sound so absurd?

So that you won't say "peace" and run away...

I thought that it would be easy.

Like they say a beach is breezy,

but it not working out quite that way.

I discovered my error in my sheer terror...

Now my pain from your distance won't go away.

Now, I am awake to my fate.

Regretfully living my mistake.

You decided to go... I should have said no...

Now my soul is ready for the grave.

Our shells turn to dust,

believe if you must.

My love will find

you again someday…

KK Rice

What Are You Thinking?

What a place we've descended

to as people of the United States.

All the problems we have fought

so long and worked hard through,

have somehow ended up back on our plate.

I am aghast that young American men

mask a love for a return of the Nazi State.

In the Father Land that crazy man's plans

are banned in any public debate.

But somehow that old evil.

Though it seems quite surreal,

reappeared into supposedly

the lovers state.

As crazy as that story, there is something else

that tarnishes our glory.

I fear that this country still treats

black men like runaway slaves.

As the Police state in Minnesota,

killed a black man because he doesn't wanna,

calm down from officer stepping on his face?

Let's trace back because it is prudent,

Black Lives Matter is a reboot of

a previous civil rights movement

where young people sat in, then marched,

were hit with water hoses, bit by dogs.

All in the Jim Crow days, 50 years ago.

We were marching for the same cause,

just pause... you can't see... we in 21st century,

you mean after an Obama we still not seen as human beings?

That's just rude! What are you talking about dude?

You see these crazy people replaced a swastika with the letter Q?

How crude. On January 6th they

thought they would rule.

But they got trumped, when he got dumped

by the conscious people of the Red White Blue.

KK Rice

Miss You Everyday

I miss you babe. There is nothing to say.

I had to play sad songs today. It made me

feel you were close and not away...

I think back to what we did wrong.

I know at first our love was so strong.

Now look at me giving it up. When we met,

I was giving you change for the ice cream truck.

I'm stuck. On memories like this.

When I made you happy with a simple wish.

To be together till whenever. We decide when the

ever is better for us to believe a spirit to whisper,

when to break us up. I need you more than ever I did.

Trying to live this life on the grid.

I did, but not so successful.

This life alone is a tussle.

Let's hustle for the things we need... working together as a family.

So, see, it just you and me.

None of these chicks or dudes across the street.

I read, my love letters you sent to me.

Being so sweet and tender, my heart needs this, you see.

I want to stay committed to you even if you don't agree.

KK Rice

Wrong One

I am so incredibly hurt that you flirt

and made love with another man.

I feel stupid in a way only a man can...

all this time I am thinking of you,

and you sleeping with him, just you two.

You let him touch you where

I have dreamed every day to let him see

what I always have tried to sneak to see.

And hide my feelings so you won't think less of me.

I am enraged at the thought that you were with him.

That man is a pure simpleton... he could not have put thought

in how to pleasure you. He only focused on his lust

with his trusts into your deep essence of your inner heart.

Not a place he ever deserved to be a part. Now he is part

of your history and I am not. I am just a chapter in another story...

If I could, I would hunt him down. For taking what I

was building in my heart as a crown... I am sick to

my heart that this news is a part of my day...

I guess it is a lesson to say my feelings right away.

If you knew how I felt. I tell myself. You would not have given that away...

If you knew then you would stay away from him.

But you were kept in the dark. I was stark in my feeling for you.

Try to hide my spark that was only for you. It not fair the things

that have happened in your life. You deserve some real love

despite any mistakes in direction of affection to someone.

Who won't pay attention to your

special needs, other than orgasms.

I am such fool I should have been

more real with you. I have so little left to lose.

From my little ruse.

KK Rice

Lost

I can't say when. I lost so many friends.

People who I loved dearly to the end.

Life has become so jaded, faded, digital and coarse,

people lose friends and no longer feel remorse.

How can you love a friend and

block them on the count of 10?

Perhaps we are seeking friends far too quickly?

Is this something we don't need to do weekly?

Then when their personality doesn't fit our style,

we fake a smile and reconcile, why suddenly

we don't talk to them decently.

We live in a great age of diversity.

Different people different cultures becoming one tree.

But notice consequently we also lost a touch of our humanity,

through the embrace of our technology. Like and block,

we do this freely.

What does it mean to hit these buttons on the screen?

5000 digital friends and personally know three?

Goodbye dear friends. I am first to admit a fault,

not only will I burn a bridge, but I'll wait until you are on it.

KK Rice

The Only Rap

I am back again. This time to win. Whatever it takes. Fuck the past mistakes. Bet the stakes. Not a winner, winner, keep that chicken dinner. I am trying to become an icon, some next level shit you ain't on. You are too narrow minded, you been blinded, silenced, sideline dead. Never reach your potential peak.

Cause you too weak. No school you a fool don't even know how to use a tool. Boo hoo. I'll see you later. Tic Tock goes the clock and as predicted with time I find you in cell 2 H Block. Nigga you were just a fool. I tried to tell you. But you only listened to the WU... but look dude. They rich and you are living in the zoo... a caged animal. All right bro I'll get you out... don't shout. I'll help you restore your clout. In the family and on the block. We've all had hard knocks.

Back to me on my feet still running to be free. Being brave, run all day... too much like a runaway slave. Not looking back, can't take me back, hoping the evil swine, won't shoot me in the spine. Wait the flip side. Ran my best. Hid my best. Didn't talk to nobody when even at rest. But then I guess I committed a crime. When I took my time at the 7 11 line.

I had picked up a coke, got a half smoke, got me some bread, cause I kind of like toast. Then some rookie had the gun to my head. Stood fast while they read some rights, they say I had. It was sad. So, I got mad. Enough to resist arrest just a tad. My no clout mouth wouldn't stop my shout. Then the 38s came out. Shot to death. Only heard the gunshots blast. The die is cast. Oblivion... not speaking of the Tom Cruise flick. But the bullets from that PD dick. That was all. Now my fall. Life is stalled. Good people I hope are appalled... call up New York News 1... Y'all... do a story no one thinks is fun... the end of this black man's epic run... the story becoming a bad re-run... quarterly... they think being black is disorderly. How do we look for new life? Keep up the fight? Finally get our earned civil rights! Teach to build the flame and protect the light. Peace

KK Rice

A Happiness Renewed

It makes me so happy to see you smile again.

I thought your time with me left your life in ruin.

Since you were gone you have blossomed so fast...

in the end I guess I was acting like a jackass.

It is certainly a possibility that I just wasted your time.

Time is a commodity that we hold very tight.

It can be the difference in living slow or at the speed of light.

My only thrill is to see you living your best life so free.

I just wish you could cope to spend your life with me.

We start a new season of love and special care.

We find a way to get each other's

back and always be aware.

I want you to be happy, especially with me.

We need to step outside ourselves and help

the other person achieves. When we find a way

to love like this, life will be so sweet.

KK Rice

Pray

I miss you so much. It's hard to believe

you don't see me just walk around on my knees.

Because every day I pray you will return your love to me.

While here I plan to give all the love you need.

Know my speech seems cheesy

and you heard it all before. But I bet you never

heard it from a man kneeling on the floor.

Looking up at you, feeling my love burn at its worst.

Give me just one second to recite these lines

I recently rehearsed. Oh, how do I love thee,

let me count the words. How many words

could I possibly say before I sound a bit absurd?

But I am willing to stay in this position.

I am praying that the gods above will bless us

with a beautiful reconciliation.

Come along with me... take my hand...

Now fly...

Everything in the world is ours, the limit is just the sky.

KK Rice

The Solid

I don't know what I did, for you

to decide so early to quit.

You came to me to bear your thoughts

of what you needed to be legit.

I stepped back at first, then I relented

to see the clear benefit. To be with someone

who loves and wants me and possibly pays half the rent?

You claimed to see all my problems and want to fix them with me.

That works, so naturally. You and I agree.

The two of us with love and trust can conquer anything.

I opened my heart halfway, it was for you to come midway

so we could connect.

When I looked around, you were not to be found

and running while screaming you regret.

I felt low and used up. Put some change in my tin cup.

With tears I looked straight up. "Why? Why? Why? Have thou forsaken me?"

God said, "Nah son. I hooked you up."

KK Rice

Falling For You - London

The first time I was in love with you.

We were in London walking the

narrow streets 2 by 2.

The sun was grey as we entered the tube.

So crowded the station

I had to embrace you.

Your dark eyes just sucked me

in your deep deep soul.

We kissed then missed our

stop at London Bridge.

You laughed then kissed me deeply

on lips and said chill out and don't you quib.

Let's get off and enjoy our day.

Walk along the river Thames

in the London rain.

We walked for hours that day.

Our Burberry's verses the rain.

All I can remember is loving

you in a special way.

We got to Chinatown in the

West End on Gerrard.

We were tired and later

we would take a black car.

Had some tea, enough for three,

then headed back to our little hotel the Grand Royale.

In our tiny room we embraced

and started to spoon.

Then on the next day we woke at noon.

Enjoyed that sausage, tea and macaroons.

Then a trip to the Eye, be quick,

see above London in the afternoon.

It was a thrill to share that experience

with you. To travel and see something new.

Funny, because I now see why the dish

ran away with the spoon.

To have good memories

with my true love, only you.

KK Rice

The Lost

How did I find you then lose you all in one day?

What did my soul do to chase you away?

I swear I was completely in love with you...

I would take a test to show it's true.

In my public displays of affection on you, was to only

explain to others how I felt about you.

You were special to me in so many ways

that no one could invade the space.

I made in my heart for you.

You were the reason to wake up before noon.

The reason to be a slave for you...

your love became my food.

I reach out in the dark, blind with

desperate arms, flailing for you.

When we in a crowd I want to be cuffed to you.

Work to make a happy life with you.

I just need to find you.

I want to remind you,

you once said you forgive

babies and fools.

KK Rice

It's OK

I am not going to lose any more of you,
I will find the hole you are leaking from
and seal it up with the truth.
I will cup my hands together and drink
as much of you as I can.

Before you spill into the ground
never to be sipped again.
My lies and my misdeeds put
the hole in the love jar
that held who we are.

Now you are leaking away
how much is left, is less than
I need, to my dismay.
I can't believe I let our
love go this way.

While I am at the jar trying to
keep you from flowing away.
I will say a prayer, that I can save at
least one cupped hand of you
and that will be ok.

KK Rice

IG Story

Hashtag this.

I don't want to be on this quest.

I am not about to zoom chat to be in love

with you, that corner has been turned.

In my heart you clearly burn.

All I think about is you.

In case you haven't got a clue.

Yeah, I said you.

I really don't care about your dude...

he a walking joke on smoke he

like too much dope.

I hope he's never woke.

Yeah, the other day he came to me

and we spoke, about you're his girl

and he not remote.

Not breaking up... ha, I think he is waking up.

Now he knows, I love you.

He can deny it till he turns blue.

You're my girl and that nothing new.

Been talking to you since last June.

Now he about to get tuned up.

Thinking I am a punk,

who gets shook up.

Let me tell you something dude.

You about to take a nap...

the kind where your eyes are X's,

I hope you get the message...

make no mistake.

I will, I take her away,

while you are none the wiser.

There is no way I will retire.

She is the only woman...

I desire.

You spent your time on PS5

and now your grip on her

has expired. Basically, you are fired.

No more talk, you just sound tired.

KK Rice

My Brown Girl

My girl is so brown, and I confound
her honey skin cannot just be found
on any girl just around.

Eyes so brown, they make me weak.
They are the color that
makes you seek.

The bottom of her soul and
the top of her heart, a more beautiful
journey you could never chart.

So beautiful is this girl.
The way she floats while taking a walk
reminds me of angels, that's real talk.

If she's what's in heaven that awaits.
I will take my life right away.
I need that glow it keeps me safe.

It makes those chicken heads run away.
Let them run off.
I got my girl in their place.

I am blessed in so many ways.

KK Rice

I Blame You For The Darkness

You gave me so much dark for my heart.

I can't live... pain is so sharp...

I wanna dig a shallow grave.

For my heart and my soul and

memories of what I did...

I need more room to find the light.

Fix my wrongs make things right.

Make a spark in the dark.

Go take a walk, in the winter park.

It was your cold heart that

made my noble heart dark.

KK Rice

Lips

My God your lips.

I would make a trip. A million miles,

in a ship, to kiss them once lovingly.

I can't resist your soft full lips honestly.

I can't lie. It doesn't hurt my pride,

to say I could die, after kissing your lips, quite happily.

What steps must I take. How much of my mortal soul

must I trade, to make you happy so you would.

Make me your slave for the curves

and dips of your beautiful lips?

I can only pray there will come a day,

when your lips call my name so I can claim another kiss just the same.

Your kiss brings peace to my soul.

How I survived before I don't know.

In my darkest dreams and darkest nights,

a kiss from you would wake me up and bring the light.

Like a star born a 100 centuries ago.

The light is the past. But never gets old.

KK Rice

TJB (The Juxtaposed Bind)

Is there a place in your heart, I can't be?

A forbidden area that I cannot be free.

An area that you once built for me and

I had decorated the walls with pictures of we.

I also painted the walls with my love can you see?

It had a window to let in the light from you through.

I made a garden and planted the seeds of the future I see.

Beautiful flowers then grew for me.

I picked them slowly and

placed them into a vase carefully.

I went to the well that went down to your heart...

to get some love so the flowers could start to

open buds that would have your fragrance I love.

Then I noticed that the flowers were drying up.

Dying of the tragedy of there was no love in the vase, I believed, I had filled up.

With weeping eyes, I ran to the well,

to my surprise, it was now completely dry.

I looked around desperately and wondered why.

Come to find out it was your ire,

you simply had no more desire, to let me live in your heart.

Then you hired two big guys named

NO and MORE to move me out,

they came to my space and threw me out.

I tried to fight back, but they said I was wack.

I had to go, or they will attack with hurtful words and a foot on my back.

I looked down and saw the vase on the ground

and all your pictures were torn down and

all the walls I painted were now brown.

I clenched up and with angry rage

I said, "What the fuck?"

I was restrained, by the two who said shut up

or we will take our time to rough you up.

The mistress said to get your butt out

of here and that it's your tough luck

you're not welcome, hear?

They said don't linger they agreed

I looked like a class 5 clinger,

so it seems. I looked at my hand

and gave them the middle finger,

after all I felt for you. (Cue in the Blues singer)

I was the fool. So silly, I became a mule.

Trying to be close to you, you got tired,

you said we were finished, thus your ire,

close the book, time to accept the truth.

I just mean nothing to you.

KK Rice

Stop The Chase

I won't chase you anymore.

You made it clear, you don't want me at all

I had my time and now it passed.

There is no reason to add a task.

I am an anchor.

But you are not at sea,

I pull you down when you want to be free.

If nothing else, I feel like a disease.

From which there is no vaccine.

I wanted to infect you like you infected me.

I believe it called in love disease.

Once exposed it spreads very quickly.

To my head and then my toes.

My mind totally froze.

In my chest my heart won't rest, I can barely breathe.

Don't see why you won't love me.

Basically, I hate the chase, loathe the race,

in my mouth it leaves a bad taste.

All my love is going to waste.

I don't think I can wait, without rest to my spirit and still have faith.

That it will all work out one day,

it will all work out one day,

it will all work out one day,

it will all work out one day.

My heart echoes like an empty cave.

KK Rice

7 Mile Run

Your legs so long my resistance

falls when I see you, instantly.

How can I steal a moment to feel,

my fingers across your knee?

I know that you must figure

the lust factor is triggered whenever

dealing with me. Just know that my stance

is to wait for my chance to love you respectfully.

Never have I seen a silhouette so pristine

as your legs in the southern light.

You had a great tan and proceeded to ran

faster than I could ever run.

It was just what you need,

to have this great speed,

So, your heart is not taken for fun.

But still I don't believe seeing your epic speed.

In one minute, 7 miles you did run.

You did it with ease and only to tease

7 miles of legs in a single leap.

You ran into the sun and looked back to see you won.

As all the men chasing you collapsed at your feet.

But it wasn't fun because there was not one

prepared to step up to your dismay. You shrugged and then

sighed then turned not satisfied.

Grabbed your pride and just walked away.

KK Rice

I Am So In Love

Babe, I am so in love with you... I want to express my loving ways

I want to convince you to stay, I pray you love me too.

Babe I just want to hold you, wrap my arms and legs around you.

I want to feel your warmth I want to be strong, so you know I adore you...

Babe, I want to lay face to face with you.

I want to share this space with you. I want to feel your hair, put it behind your ear.

So, I can whisper how much I love you.

Babe, I want to spoon with you.

I want to do it very soon. I want you to feel my hold, I want you to behold,

how your love can make my heart chained to you.

Babe, I don't want to let go of you.

I been lonely in the past and it won't do.

Just let me hear your voice. I not giving you a choice,

this is what lovers do.

Babe, I want to make life plans with you.

I just can't stand to be without you.

My future used to look grey, there is nothing more to say,

I am free for the next century or two.

Babe, all that I am is because of you.

I fight what they call the MAN for you.

When it 6 AM I set my heart to win. So, I can build my home with you.

Babe, I hope you know how much I need you. I hope you need me too.

You made my life begin I hope it never ends because I want to see it through.

Babe, we have beautiful babies,

we do, here is baby one, now two.

We are going live this life, yeah it will be a fight,

the world versus just us two.

Babe, I want to pass away with you.

I want to hold each other and never move. After 90 years came last week,

I think that time is a thief, but our love had just barely peaked,

and God must have seen our love so deep.

He stopped for a moment so he can weep and

took us both so we can share our eternal sleep.

Babe, I think we made it thru...

the pearly gates and angel wings for two...

now we can always dance, continue our romance,

babe I don't want to be ever without you.

God knows I love you.

KK Rice

King

You are a mom to a prince not seen

since the time of our people on the Nile.

Though you been through fire,

I admire your desire, to raise you son

with the pride of an Egyptian pharaoh.

It will be fast time but within your Timeline

before your son is ready to sing...

He will be tall and broadside with

a hand he will arise, and his tune will

be Honor thy King.

I am old and finished but one of my last wishes

is to see all the sons of the motherland reclaim their crown.

All the strife of today is just to distract and dissuade.

Our sons for succeeding at life and the sick game.

But after knowing his mom, this plan they have will bomb.

And your son will be part of the black consciousness army brigade.

KK Rice

Don't Play Me

I have no choice, I lost the voice,
that would have created the boundary
between your coarse and misplaced
feelings that I am your enemy.

The boundary works in line to define
that part of my heart that shows my vulnerabilities.
The facts persist, though I resist that
feeling to love you like this.

To give you my time,
not measured by a dime,
but if it was, we both would be rich.
You spat callous thoughts that were.

Darkly wrought with so many inaccuracies.
It makes me think while making my heart sink.
The fact that you never really loved me.
In the speech you served, why did I deserve?

Clarity to your disenchantment with me.
My only grace, with you is to say I am sorry.
I made it my base, and this pertains to your case,
that everyone deserves a chance to save face.

As so their image is not defaced in the
warm memories I have in place in my mind.
However, don't be blind, it is a rare find to have this level
of love given to those who are not blood.

If it happens again.

I say if and not when.

You will only see my sword and not the dove.

KK Rice

Cosmic Additions

The universe can't live without our souls

which gives it goal to be beautiful and bold.

It is the beats of our hearts made from the same parts

as the cosmos that make the earth orbit around its own star.

In a years' time we will find that our journey around

comes back to the beginning.

The human mind always sees time in straight lines.

We start in the past and go forward so fast until.

Our bodies just stop breathing.

As are our only perception of time being

to be born once, live and then die.

Is it a thought that can be quite foreboding?

It takes an open mind to think perhaps we move in time,

just like earth moves around in a circle,

which is why we sometimes whine because

from time to time it feels like fears we had once thought.

The dead and past come back to feed on the living.

KK Rice

Confusion

I write so much poetry and now I realize why.

My heart been broken down deep inside.

My mind and soul are not well, it started

to spell certain sadness and weakness to my will.

Though partially just made of pride.

I decided to hide, foolishly, my sadness inside

and now it has capsized my truths and roots

of what was told to me. From the age three.

None of the presumptions including faith

have made the safe horizons by then.

I am no longer hiding what

I feel to make real...

KK Rice

Tickle Me Please

Tickle me please so I can laugh

Tickle me please so I scream

Tickle me please so I know I am not a dream

Tickle me please so I can't breathe

Tickle me please so I can feel your touch

Tickle me please so I won't feel a rush

Tickle me please so I can beg you to stop

Tickle me please so I know you will not

Tickle me please so your heart won't forget me

Tickle me please so your emotions won't regret me

Tickle me please so I can feel your truth

Tickle me please you're my only roots

Tickle me please so I can see the love you have for me

Tickle me please I don't have COVID-19

Tickle me please so these ties will bind

Tickle me please so I won't go blind

Tickle me please so alone is not what I will be

Tickle me please my soul is built like a fort

Tickle me please in my heart I must now sort

Tickle me please for our weekly rapport

Tickle me please as a last resort.

………. Sorry I must pee!

KK Rice

Failure Creates

I failed at this, I failed at that.

What can I see? I can't turn back.

Time only moves one way.

You can make the future brighter but give up yesterday.

Every day I wake, arm myself to take,

a wider stake in my own fate.

I look for the date when the world will rate

when I finally state my intentions.

Put the world on fire with my creative desire,

to make all things beautiful with my direct attention.

Life is bright and can only be right when you have great jubilation.

For me it's easy to see those who enjoy that which I created.

Yet still one more try there are those who would die

to stop all my concentration. To plan my new way to make

a display of all my surreal inventions.

KK Rice

To Hell

I regret the night you left in flight.

My heart rushed to hold you tight...

you moved so fast. As fast as light.

And I was alone the rest of that night.

I called you once it didn't connect.

I called again I became a wreck.

One more try and I almost died

until you answered and said goodbye.

I took your words to wish me well.

With my one ticket to my lonely hell.

When I got to gate Satan took me in quick.

He said this line please just for you dicks.

Just I figured clear as a bell you

mean what you said... go to hell.

They gave me my horns then my three headed stick.

Stuck on a tail. With a glue stick... I was all dressed.

Just like a prick. Go out and cause hell, the red lord spoke,

fire and nails make sure it sticks.

The devil looks at me with an uncertain grin,

shook his head, then he began,

all my minions will do their hell work.

But the deal I struck with your lord said you would stay put.

You had to come here you earned that spot,

but you are not to walk the earth again.

The hope is you will rot.

The world had an enough

of you as a misanthrope.

KK Rice

Regret

I can't stand there is no plan for us

to be together anymore.

Your stand against my last plan led to a bloody war.

A battle I had no right to fight but

you would continue to even the score.

The only weapons I weld to fight is my heart, my soul.

I hit what I can keep in my sights.

The weapons you used were far more

powerful, unexpected, yet very logical.

Distance, resistance, your steadfast persistence

not to acknowledge my existence, broke all my defenses.

I raise my white flag. I surrender all I have. Was I that bad?

I launched at you love, I launched at you respect

and I haven't used any reinforcements yet.

Going to keep loving you until you just give up.

There is no defense from common sense

even when I have screwed up.

Open your walls and you will see.

I only bring with me peace.

You have a look I haven't taken any of your ease.

Peace with me will allow me to please everything you want.

I just want to end a war

that probably started

because I was a punk.

KK Rice

Medication

Pills, pills, pills. Every morning when sun is dawning...
I take my 7 pills to life that is drawing down my will
to fight. It's not right, I feel like I can't sleep most nights.

Let me tell you what I fear. My mind in the morning
not being there, then being buried dead in this sphere.
I hear my love she is near, I see she casts a soft tear.

She remembers when I had no fears and
mostly laughed if death was near.
Now death has moved in, it occupies the space I live in.

When it comes to put my ills to rest,
it is the pills that save my breath,
I can tell what's left is a bitter hardened shell.

I picture of when I once was well.
Losing my mind with all my soul, no longer bold,
death has a trick when it learns what you hate well.

Let's tell you a lie,
say no to what keeps you alive,
even if that is God or pills.

KK Rice

The End Of "We"

I am not who you thought,

you are not who I thought,

there is no reason to continue as "we".

"We" never agree or even succeed in

loving each other happily.

It is time to be sound and start a rebound.

Because our little bit of love is just not enough.

Just get your stuff. No, you don't need to rush.

But I think it is clear "we've" had enough.

"We" wanted to see before we retreat if our

blood bond of little feet will bring us closer naturally.

But little souls should not be told they needed for their elder's well being.

Better to be alone to grieve than wear a mask that is not to be believed.

She responds, "We agree, foolish me."

KK Rice

Inside A Wreck

Why can't I keep the tears out of my eye?

I can't control my fears, can I?

They are eating me alive like a cancer inside.

That how I watched my father die.

Just saw the life chased from his eye.

I think he wanted me to see that life was meant to be treated as a 1st prize.

I wake and often despise, the feeling, I am lost despite,

I am in my own bed. Not even close to dead.

But still not showing my best person Instead.

Instead, I just play dead. I am only close to a few.

I was wrong to make this a rule. I am a limited man.

I have a new road to cross.

As I navigate a brand-new course.

I smile and wave to begin a new way to

win without all my heavy sins.

It's a coin toss. Heads I win, means tails pain and fear

would have lost now I am the boss of all things me,

just call it my destiny. Live as if you never have sinned.

I lift the weight so I can freely breathe again.

KK Rice

Dammit

DAMMIT! DAMMIT! I must start a Monday.

DAMMIT! DAMMIT! It is my most hated day.

DAMMIT! DAMMIT! There is always a staff meeting on this day.

DAMMIT! DAMMIT! What was wrong with Wednesday?

DAMMIT! DAMMIT! Where the hell is this stupid train?

DAMMIT! DAMMIT! Just 4 more days to my vacay.

DAMMIT! DAMMIT! I want to be rich as shit one day.

DAMMIT!! DAMMIT!! If you work in NEW YORK,

like the Mob, you can't just walk away.

KK Rice

GF Justice

Such a relief to finally see justice
delivered equally, not just based
on the color of skin, you see.

I am praying that the next officer of the PD.
Will resist the temptation to use his knee
while ordering a man to his feet.

Blindly confusing resistance with not being able to breathe.
Finally, it's clear for all to see, what black men must fear,
just walking down, the street.

Justice for all is this country's creed with
a dash of freedom should be all men
need to have the privilege of their humanity.

KK Rice

Run (Song I)

I want to run.

Really run away.

I want to run.

Starting this very day.

I want to run.

I have this feeling every day.

I want to run.

Unless you think it best to stay?

I want to run.

I don't even know the names.

I want to run.

Of those who want to be delayed.

I want to run.

Toward the bay of south Biscayne.

I want to run to the sun and catch some rays...

I want to run.

For too long my soul been put away.

I want to run.

It has led to my decay.

I want to run.

Covid deaths every day.

I want to run.

To breathe the air again.

I want to run.

I got my shot to be prepared.

I want to run.

To see the world once again.

I want to run.

It has been a human toll.

I want to run.

from the people who think the election had been stolen.

I want to run.

To the truth so it can be really told.

I want to run.

This feeling is just too new.

I want to run.

From the people worshiping a Q.

I want to run.

When I was young it was fun.

I want to run.

I am tired now I am done.

KK Rice

My Son

It is my time to rest my son.

It is my time just be able to sit in the sun.

The world I built is now yours to make

it rich or poor. It's time to find what's yours.

I don't want you to be sad my son.

In my mind I have only won.

I see you now you so tall.

Still remember when you were small.

Still looking at me to show you more.

I gave you all the best of me.

After some time,

I hope you will see.

I've only shown you faith.

How not to hate.

How to use more than your eyes to see

and with your mind to create beautiful dreams.

I see my darkness coming near, my son.

The light starts to fade,

it only goes away when I am done.

It going to be alright, this is the circle of life my son.

I wouldn't want to change a thing,

not one. Boy just rest me here.

I want my lungs to feel the last of fresh air.

I think the weather will be fair.

Just going to sit in this chair.

You go and find some fun.

It nice to be young my son.

Chase the pretty girls that run.

Study all the books before fun.

Get a skill that will hook.

The sweet life you want.

One more thought my son.

As I see the last of the sun.

I want you always to be.

From inside very happy.

Find a love that sets you free.

The horror of life is that it wants the dark.

It wants you to sleep and play a part.

Keep the light in your heart brighter than a star.

Don't give up on yourself at all.

KK Rice

My Foot Taste Bad

Lord, you must be tired of me constantly

asking for what I don't need.

I don't need a million dollars,

or a red Ferrari, a house in the Caribbean,

or be around beautiful woman. That I would start pinching.

No, what I need is a release.

A moment to find my spiritual peace.

Can we arrange a time to discuss these

ideas at your earliest convenience?

God heard my lazy plea,

and took his time to answer dryly.

He replied, "There is no question where I reside,

peer into your heart and I am there you will find.

But if you need something less broad in scope.

Check the building across

the street with the cross, just go.

I am there every day twice, even on Sunday.

Can you manage in your schedule

to give me even one day?"

God sat and rested his knee

then he continued talking to me.

"Man is so crazy to me, but let me ask a question.

Man can find time to be anywhere,

some places that just lead to your despair.

But not come to a place that can give you life

and all my heavenly care?"

SMH "Word!" I said realizing I am joke. Next time

I will think my words rather than have stupidly spoken.

Realizing my mistake, I stepped back to restate

to God please excuse my dance as I took a chance

that you would not notice my absence from your view.

In my heart and your church, I agree is the best search

and going forward I will work to merge my body with my

spiritually so I can find what is

most important to me.

Peace

KK Rice

Making Love

I wish with all my heart that I can give you

the million stars in the dark.

The fire of the cosmos I want to impart.

Then my love, all the rivers, oceans

and seas would be yours.

With them all the beautiful shores.

Next the forests and mountains would be named after you.

A majestic thought

I think that is new.

We would live in Paris

and vacation as we please.

Sail in a yacht in your namesake seas.

All I can see is that wind in your hair.

The sun in your eye and

a bikini that don't care.

Everyday dawn would be a new view.

An exotic port or a new beach or two.

Give me a year with nothing to do but rub some love and sun lotion on you.

All my fantasies are growing old with you.

Still making love when we are in the mood.

The world won't believe what they see.

So, in love it's embarrassing.

PDA every chance I get. Better get set to protect your neck.

How did something so beautiful end up with me.

Oh, I see, this a dream.

KK Rice

Despise I

I look in your eyes now and all I see is the
hate and distrust you have of me.
I can't approach you without your jump.
I can't speak to you without you
thinking I am a punk.

I can't touch you without
you wanting to punch.

I am sorry that we have gone this horrible path.
But darkness falls and always like that.
Lovers who are now strangers,
there is no going back.

We let a long lie take over our lives,
now it is alive and eats our ties.

I don't know how we shoulder
this miserable yoke, so tight on our neck
we daily choke on simple words,
I like, I love you are never spoken as a rule.

So sad we live this lonely life.
Two feet away but no love in sight.
How long can we live by just being polite?
A nod and a grunt each at morning's light.

I never thought I could live this way before.
I know for you it must be a chore.
I am not a devil or angel of pain.
But at some point, we can't stay sane.

I am not sure if there is a need for anymore talk.

I will get some things and just take a walk.

KK Rice

My Sprit

Over some time, I have come to believe

that I can string together words beautifully.

But admittedly this day I have a stall.

Realizing how much your beauty calls.

To my eyes and my heart without apart

from the ways you make the days seem hot.

I sweat my desire to light a fire that burns for you.

Inside here without fear of being burned by you.

Where there is smoke there is fire,

but not to expire our dreams prior

to living a long life with you and me.

And once we die and pass the fire to those we leave in our place.

It will only mean we leave these corporeal beings

and our spirits will ring into infinity,

while moving at the speed of light,

if we are wrong, or right,

I remain at your side faithfully.

KK Rice

Life Change

My life one night changed forthright
without a doubt in my mind.
Despite my assets I found my
attachment to you is unrefined.

What learned in time that I can't rewind?
My life even for a few moments.
Mostly I can't deny that my life is behind
without you in my arms or presence.

It is what we see as people you and me,
what it means to be wealthy or poor.
Truth be dammed I lost all that I had.
The day you walked out the door.

Now every night before I sleep tight,
I pray to God to bring you back complete.
Like a small child I weep before I sleep because
my mind can't accept, I lost what I once had.

God just smiled after I sat for a while
and said, son, why do weep like this so?
I put it in print and I won't relent when I said
you reap what you sow.

Why did you give up what you had in the cup?
To drink deeply love to quench your blood thirst,
I will never cosign on your thoughts to be blind
to what you gave to her in a world of hurt.

She prayed to me several times on what
her heart should do with you.
My only advice to her suffice.

Was to go, so to survive your torture.

You had no right to be like the night.
And frighten her like a little girl.

KK Rice

My Love 1 (Song 2)

I hope, I never forget to say I love you.

I hope, you always want me to say it to you.

Through the toughest years and the painful tears

I am here, and I still love you.

I am only a simple man. I do what most men can.

Without my better half, the world would sit and laugh.

Shake their head and say what a fool.

They don't know what it means to love you.

They don't know what it means to adore you.

We have simple magic that why it so tragic,

if we change the way it feels between us two.

Nothing bears my cross, from a simple loss of your love and heart deep from in you...

I am not a perfect man,

but my love I have a plan.

And that is to stay in love with you.

You can try to leave. But it is a guarantee,

my love will find a way to you.

Hold my hand to see that I love you.

There is not another man. That will ever say this to you.

The sun and moon set and rise

with your enchanting eyes and

through it all this much is true.

You can search the cosmos, but I am telling you that I'm the most.

The one that's most in love with you.

KK Rice

Despise II (Song 3)

Hate you?

My God no! How can I hate such a beautiful soul?

Hate you?

My God why? How can I hate what's been the apple of my eye?

Hate you?

My god is this a joke?

I love you so much it hard not to choke.

Hate you?

My God how?

There is no one else I want to be with right now.

Hate you?

MY GOD stop kidding.

The desperate acts of love we do are generally forbidden.

Hate you?

My God don't be silly.

My love for you will run into infinity.

Hate you?

My God! My love!

For the next 1000 years you will never get the sword, just the dove.

Hate you?

My God you are lost?

It wasn't I who took our love and gave it a vengeful toss.

Hate you?

My God I wouldn't force it is you who after all we had that wanted a divorce?

Hate you?

Well let me think. According to this report you give too many guys a wink.

Hate you?

It is becoming a little clearer. I followed you and saw you two kissing in the rearview mirror.

Hate you?

Stop fronting! I see you getting your hair done and to the store to get you something.

Hate you?

Honestly, I am not impressed, you can't even come home without a wrinkled dress.

Hate you? Why? I have no grounds I heard about your escapades all over town.

Hate you?

I can't recall. Any other time I've been absolutely appalled.

Hate you?

Yup.

KK Rice

Love Instead

I no longer want to play my part.

With this life of my heart in the dark.

I want to breathe the air that we share

and let the light pierce my dark fears and not care.

All I wanted was to love you, but I only caused tears

and leers to the side of eyes focused on my hands

and my plans to be with you... What part did my heart

play in this sort of damaged state of being?

It was sacrificed to briefly feel what it would be to be in love with you.

If only for a day. I would make my way just to say I love you.

The heart was taken, my blood mistaken for tears of sadness on the floor.

That was believed to be only about leaving me.

But it was my soul. That still fights and still believes the

love you once breathed into there exists.

Despite the risks to fail to make it worth your time.

Not looking to hide my faults to you anymore.

But to settle the score. 0 to 1 yours.

Is there more to reveal, even steal in these hands

that hold my torn-up soul together with nothing but fear and string

but not nicer things. Like beauty and love.

Not the sword but the dove.

I used to convince you to love me once again.

The plan it's a sin. But how can I win?

You made me happier than I had ever been.

All that, as I feared, was taken with you as you moved away like the wind.

KK Rice

My Love I

Is there any way not to dream about your body next to me?

How can get my daily sleep when all I do is dream about you? Sweets.

I can't explain how this fire for you started,

I can only allow it to foster, into giant blaze of orange and red glaze

the heat of 1000 suns.

Or even how lava runs, freely over life and trees,

totally burned at a million degrees.

That is the fire that I see for you and me.

Please don't tease me with another man in my seat,

holding hands with your skin tan and salty. But tastes sweet.

With sword in hand, I protect your heart from evil clans,

of dishonest men who never begin to even chart

what makes you a whole woman with a golden heart.

For this, I can never be apart.

Am a knight of the light never the dark.

KK Rice

Hold Un To My Heart. A Love Epic. (Song 3)

Do you remember the day you left me? That's the same day my sad soul died. Just got up and left without me. I didn't know the reason why. Did you think I would be lonely? Did you even really care? When I was scared, you wrap your arms around me. And we just let evil stare... there's so much I could tell you, what has happened all these years. I couldn't fully replace you. Honestly, I wouldn't even dare. If you fully see me. What's in my heart is so pure. I'll tell you a little secret... from your venom there was no cure.

You left me to die, I always wondered why you needed to? Was your soul entwined with other dimes, I wasn't good enough? If you're so blind to leave me behind, then I had enough. Just keep in mind, the hateful crime that you had to do. Take the knife. Twist it twice. Just to make sure. You kill me nice, don't think why, don't let me live anymore. Without your love or tender touch. On my weakened soul, there is no dawn or reason to prolong my heart anymore. With no love to claim, it just the same to live with your disdain.

Do want me to give up on you. I will no longer waste my time. It takes too long to get into you, if you just make up your mind. I know you used to love me. I know I used to be your dear. Black tears flow down right through me; my screams I know you can hear. Just like swimming in an ocean, when there is no sight of a pier. I have no place for rescue. So, I just coldly die right here. My body sinks to the bottom of this ocean named for you. How was I to know, I was sinking? When I was yelling help to you. But that day you weren't perfect. Just got finished feeling blue. Smoked a pipe full of ashes. While I was still praying for you.

Don't look at me surprised with those grey dead eyes. Hoping I will be scared you. You sooner try to stop a sunrise. Before I stop loving you. Ain't we in love? We fit like a white silk glove. Flying like a dove. I still hope for a chance, maybe for more romance. Or maybe I am still just a fool...

If you really want to leave me, pay no attention to my tears. Keep on walking, just go away, I will sit here with all my fears. You will think of my small voice. When a new love tries to come near. Put your ear to my chest and tell me what you think you hear. You may hear my torn heart beating, less and less with every tear. As my last hours passed quickly, my soul will be clear. Living with the pain that crushed me, while taking all my will to live. My heartless body could not go on. While you and Jehovah work out a secret deal.

Shock me twice to save my life. Maybe now I can heal? Breathe in life, it only right, just let me steal, the only thing I believe is real. It's your heartless kiss that I feel. Goodbye my love. Goodbye to love, there is no love, without your love. Empty heart no way to start.

KK Rice

My Love II

I still love you more than I say.

There is nothing that would take me away from your heart.

This fact you can take no part.

If you were smart you try to make me stop.

You know I am in love with your beautiful soul...

completely in love from your head down to your toes.

Your feet I would love to massage make it simple

while I try to dodge the truth. I know the source of the root.

You don't feel I can be with just you.

I am really learning my place.

I know I can no longer occupy the space.

Deep in your heart.

You won't let me to light the spark.

I want your body to be close to me.

Feel the heat generated by the concept of WE.

It won't take long to be sweet.

I think you know the old routine.

We rumble, then look in between our love and the feelings we mock...

at this point we shouldn't be shocked...

our love is still solid like a mountain top.

Yesterday I saw you walking away.

Going to visit our special spot.

I know you loved it a lot...

I sense you kind of agree.

It was the very beginning of we...

we often kiss, and we began to see...

this cold world offers nothing we really need.

Certainly not love or regard...

So we just pass and keep up our guard...

love is fragile, and is not believed by many people

who think it can't be achieved?

But I think they are just not free.

They are still a slave to the need.

For the flesh at the fastest speed.

Never thinking as us, beyond the physical sexual thrust...

they make me sad and I am so glad it not at all us.

Keep the light bright and come in from the dark.

KK Rice

In My Eye

Can I tell you, you're beautiful every day?

Can I take the privilege and say it my way?

Can I tell you that you are in my every dream?

I have of living with my love it seems.

Can I tell you this? Because, this is really me.

Can I tell you that I never really been in love before?

If I am not doing enough. Please tell me what more.

Did I tell you that you are beautiful today?

If I didn't, then I made a mistake.

There is not a time I see you when you are not beautiful to me...

I don't care what others think. I just love what I see.

I think what I view is fueled by my mood.

Every day that I wake, I know that I love you.

I woke today without time on my clock,

but I check my IG at 8 AM sharp.

I must see what story you post of you there.

A glimpse of your eyes, the flip of your hair.

500 views, yet still, I stare.

Watching you walk on a small little screen,

watching even more when I get my glasses clean.

Do you know what you do that you don't realize?

You cock your head left, when you smile.

You part your lips slightly when you are about to speak.

You give a small pause as a part of your speech.

My waiting ears that love your tough but sweet voice.

When we first met you said, "You are staring too much... you act like you lost."

In fact, I was lost. In the fog between loving you close or creating a loss.

I feel no shame, nor regret, only the sadness when you left.

You turn off your screen, no more to stream, you can't hear me scream.

At the last post for that was my dream or nightmare however it seems.

When your love walks away and can't be seen.

KK Rice

The Wall (A Lost Epic)

The wall that I see is made from fear of you and me. It was built to contain my love but was not complete in time to do the job. So, it just became a barrier that I could not leap, became an alarm if I tried to creep. The last defense before your heart. You built it well. I could not impale its strong will. I tried strong love words. I tried strong love thought... I came to the gate and even knocked. The gatekeeper looked at me through a hole, made in the door that was so strong. He asked me what I needed, what was wrong? I said I was just visiting. I didn't plan to stay long. I was walking along this road called Lovers way... I had walked it once before, with your queen, who is hidden behind your door. Back then, this great wall did not exist. Tell me gatekeeper when did you build a wall like this? The gatekeeper looked then rested his spear to the side of the door keeping it near... he stood on his toes at the hole so he could speak clear. I turned my head left. So, I could use my good ear. The gatekeeper began to tell me a story of woe, that started the day with the heart I had stolen. Do you remember so far? You came for her heart. But didn't return. She prayed for you each day from morning to dusk... then at night she would weep she missed your love so much. You gave her great love but would not give her yourself. So, one day she stood on her pride and gathered herself. She ordered the wall built with stones you left from your heart... they weighed you down from your easy depart. The mortar was mixed with water from her eyes and the tears from the rain. You made her so sad when she couldn't stand the pain. Most of her hurt was made into the mortar that was mixed with the tears or was it the water? Then the slaves that you left, true and love, built the wall strong, she liked it that way. You first came to her it was only halfway. Now you have returned with the other half far too late... behind the wall she has built a home that is good. With a man and children, I think like she hoped you would. But settle your soul to just play games... sometimes a good life comes after great pain. But this you won't see. Because she made all the sacrifices to be happy with her family. This wall is a sign for you to be reminded of what had been lost in that short time. Life makes tunnels for you to go through, some will make you very happy some will make you blue. But take the chance... walk a path. It ok if you love and become a fool. I looked at the wall and looked at the door. The hole from which the gatekeeper spoke closed without another word. I heard a loud lock, then the wrestling of a key... then a long whistle song as he walked away from me. I held my head low I leaned on the wall. I felt the tears form while I was filled with hate, for myself... when you know you love someone but let them go. How does one recover? Maybe they don't. The result of not taking that step with my heart was gaining a door with a hole, and a strong wall built around it... now I know that you must decide, bear a little pain now with years to recover. Conversely, hurt a lot later, with the time remaining of your days. Choose wisely how your life closes and the last words of your breath. The one constant of the world other than gravity is to die.

KK Rice

Gone

I didn't realize you were gone. Already done,

away from me your heart empty.

You are gone, foolish me, only now to be free.

My heart still belongs to you, but you decided you are through.

Now I am alone with no one at home.

No one to share my misery or smiles.

Healing my soul will take a while.

You are gone, so I weep, it's my fault that my heart was weak.

You told me that you were going today, but I decided not to say,

I really love you can't you see, I am nothing without you.

Even though you are more without me.

Back on your own, I am alone, a sad king on a lonely throne.

Yes, I am a king, but you were my realm.

Never more to be part of my home.

How can I live with so little to give?

All my love left with you, I did, beg your heart I remember once.

On my knees, but it is not enough.

Then twice I begged again when I had nothing to win.

When three times came. I played the game.

Wait for your heart to love me again.

It never did, now you rid, yourself from me.

Rip through my heart and what was left to see.

What can I see? What can I plea?

The only thing comes to me

is whispers from the dead dark trees.

KK Rice

I Wait A Lifetime

Can you believe, after all these years?

I still love you, despite my fears.

What do I see? that has me so scared?

I am alone, without you in my life.

Still in love but you are nowhere in sight.

I look out a window, all my hair turned grey.

Tears in my eyes, because you didn't stay.

Life can be cruel, when it makes you a fool.

So short it becomes. Before you know it, you are done.

Never having that one love in your life.

Not one.

KK Rice

Lost III

My god, do you know what I lost?

My heart, my soul, my life, laugh if you must.

You left a space that I cannot bear.

The love I had could not compare.

Say that you love and miss me too.

Say that if you could change, you would.

So I don't feel like a fool.

If I am, then let me be.

Deep in my feelings forever I see.

Let me love you, say that I can.

It the only thing that lets me live.

That was the plan. To stand without you

is like lifting a lead weight tied around my heart.

Dragging me to my fate.

I know how this road ends even if I can't admit it.

I ruined my heart for others.

So, I could let you fit in.

KK Rice

Die

I don't know how you felt before,

but I don't want us to die anymore.

I don't want you to cry anymore from the pain of you dying anymore.

Watching the flame in your eyes

just go black, makes my heart sore.

I don't want you to die anymore.

Whenever we see each other

we see death, nothing more.

I just don't want you to die anymore.

Every day seems like

more than I can endure.

But I don't want you to die anymore.

KK Rice

Why Are You Deep In My Heart?

Why are you deep in my heart?

Is it my fear of being apart?

This life that I have I can't start without you.

Because you are deep in my heart.

Why are you deep in my heart?

Is it funny to watch me stumble my words as I wish on a star?

To have you love me wherever you are?

You know I see you from afar I remember the days.

We were a part of a love thing that left a mark.

On my soul and my life. Is it just my luck that you left

when I loved you the most?

About the time you became remote.

Why are you deep in my heart?

Like a knife I twist and pull

till my blood turns red, that's

the piece you left there.

Red is the color that only means love.

I remember it well in the rose petals I would put in your tub.

That's the past and still it hurts.

I know I can only offer my flesh of my heart.

But some of the greatest stories have small starts.

KK Rice

Poets Don't Get To Love

Poets don't get to love.

They are bound to write whatever

is beyond their reach or sight.

Poets don't get to love,

if they did, the poem would

not be diverse, full of anguish, or seem more rehearsed.

Poets don't get to love,

how else can they explore your pain?

Recall your sins, know how you feel when it rains.

Poets don't get to love,

how could they impart your loneliness, jealousy or broken heart?

Know when love ends or when it starts.

Poets don't get to love,

they find religion in an unattainable condition.

Feeling the warm touch of a mutual love mission.

Poets don't get to love,

how could they seamlessly answer what you will do?

Without that one you deeply love.

The poet knows that woe.

What will you do when life goes on but live the life as bright as the sun?

Pulling in all the world has done to make it seem like you have won.

Poets don't get to love.

It is a dream that they have when they make a first draft

of words that make either sense or crap.

But either will do because

poets don't get to love

like you.

KK Rice

If Ever

If saying you are beautiful is not what you need.

Tell me what is, so I can plainly see.

If saying you are lovely crosses the line.

I will tie up my heart and leave my lust behind.

If you see me just able to stare.

It because you are so beautiful,

and none compare.

If you see weakness ever in me.

It because your sweetness just came and broke me.

I know that your heart has taken a new course.

I know it's too late. I just feel remorse...

KK Rice

I Just Weep

My love, can I say that still?

Even if your soul won't bend to my will?

Everything I've become is wrapped up in you.

Without your love, my heart doesn't move.

I am aware that I love you too much.

Now that my life can't be without your touch.

I can't believe we will go on without

sleeping in each other's arms.

Is it poor form for me to beg? For your love and not hate?

I know that my mouth said things that were a mistake.

It's only showing the fear that I have

of losing you forever, and fuels my attack.

In my heart, where my soul resides,

surrounded even now by foolish pride.

Stands to face a world alone,

wearing a lead crown by a lonely throne.

How did I ever, love you this much?

It too hard to walk, the pain of missing you is too much.

Please have some mercy, even for me.

I can't believe you don't still love our "we".

I pray for you to come back to me.

What did I do? That mistake was not me.

My heart beats blue it makes people scared.

Who am I now? I have become unaware.

Now a lonely dude with an eternal crush.

That flame will never bend. Stay burning until my end.

Twist my arm, put me in harm's way to your heart,

lock the cage door, don't let me out. Keep me

trapped in your heart.

Till I can't breathe. Smother me with love.

Until I am dead just poke me to see.

Do you love me anymore?

You just shake your head no, so I just weep.

KK Rice

I Fell In Love Once

I remember once I fell in love.

I saw your heart and I was done.

I always try to remember the most.

How I felt when you walked through my soul.

My heart once beat blue but became red.

Without you in my life I am better off dead.

Though death would be met with sadness and regret.

Without the chance of being in love with you instead.

Your eyes are so deep the blackness makes my eyes red.

Doing everything in my power to keep

my starving heart fed.

I am living off the beautiful wave that you make.

All the men pray their soul you will next take.

Do you understand how beautiful you are?

There is nothing like you until the next nearest star.

1000 years is how long it would take to make it there.

But I am willing to wait. I will pull up a chair.

I plan while I wait.

I can only do what I see is the best way

to lead into your heart.

So, I can once again breathe.

KK Rice

Her

My love, let me say that again,

if I don't say it twice,

the words on my lips

blow away with the wind.

I want my love to be real.

My heart impossible to steal,

your beautiful eyes and your lips

make my confession worth the risk.

You are so beautiful I love your

hair like the first fallen snow… so soft and light

your bang you sometimes fight.

Until it falls perfectly on your brow.

Your eyes big and round. Brown like

the rich earth in the ground.

Your body moves without a sound,

just a swish of your hips so you can get around.

Hips I wish to hold, my words

should remain untold, let my heart just explode

in silence as I just hold, what's left of me,

my poor soul… in love but not bold.

KK Rice

Hey

Do you know how badly I want to hear your Hey? It is all I want. It is all I crave.

You don't know what it means to me to get your Hey. I just pray, please look my way.

I would give you anything you say, if you would just say Hey. I will wait all day.

I would comb my hair in a different way. If I could get a Hey. Sometime today.

I would Change my Style and walk a different way... if you would just say Hey... there's no other way.

When did your Hey make me become this way? Can't let my soul decay. From my mistake.

Your hey is the best thing I have ever got. When you just say Hey, I Just feel the love a lot.

When you say hey it's not something I can throw away. I keep it safe, save it for a rainy day...

For me It seems to just rain for days. Clouds are shades of grey. Keep the sun away.

There is the message on my phone. It just says Hey. I reply, with a smiley face. It just my way.

Your hey can wake me up to seize my day, let me wash my face. Clear the sleep away.

Who taught you to say Hey in that special way? Some love from another day? Or maybe passed away?

After your hey, I wipe the tears away. If I don't hear your Hey, my eyes stay red all day.

I see you trying to keep all your Hey's. You can afford, to give one away. I don't have to pay.

I live just great from day to day, on the hey you gave, just yesterday.

Like a hero you just saved the day. Just from a Hey. Please don't fly away.

The word hey comes from ancient days. When love was made. Not just a game that was played.

To get your Hey takes the work of 1000 slaves. For 100 Days with no break.

I am ashamed that I must have your Hey. Or I will die today. There no easy way.

Please don't let me die this way. Wasn't that yesterday? When you forgot my name?

I never wanted to steal your Hey. That's not my way. That starts your hate.

Your hey has so much power. It can weigh on me or set me free.

I am Riding around town, when it hot... Looking for your Hey, in an Olds '68, green lights all the way.

Your hey seems to give me faith. So, I just pray. That I will get your Hey.

You better never think you can stop. I will go to my grave. Bury me with all my hey's.

Can't you just see I love you a lot? Tell me what's in the way. Of just getting my Hey.

Was it that I used to like to party a lot? I told you I forgot their names.

It not even the same.

They don't even want to say hey. They can go away.

I hear the phone ring, is that my Hey?

No, it's a mistake, just a Bill that's late.

I sit in my chair and just cross my legs. Until I hear your Hey, I'm just going to stay.

If you said I get no hey without giving an arm. Take my arm away I have two anyway.

If you said no hey until my hair is old and gray. Then I would wait. 1000 years to be safe and a day.

If you said no Hey until it snows in Hades. I just saw news today. Guess what they say.

Your Hey is more important than all my bones... Just my heart remains. I hope yours beats the same.

What else must I convey? I just miss your Hey... Please send it right away.

So, I can fly away, in the words you say. Just my love is safe, and my mind won't change, but I need that Hey.

On my knees, I will just pray. To hear your Hey today.

KK Rice

www.ingramcontent.com/pod-product-compliance
Lightning Source LLC
Chambersburg PA
CBHW071155130726
47998CB00002B/512